Contents

Introduction

This book examines the issues that lead to, govern and end conflicts. It explores the elements of human nature that are ready to be tapped by powerful leaders who strive for power or greater territory. The book also looks at the way in which conflicts actually take shape and grow, sometimes pitting neighbour against neighbour. Along the way it poses questions about how you, the reader, would feel in some of these terrifying situations, and what sort of measures can be taken to reduce the chance of violent conflict in the new millennium.

Causes of war

Just about everyone has had an argument with a family member, friend or even a stranger. There is usually a dispute that lies at the heart of the argument – the amount of pocket money you should be allowed, whose turn it is on a computer game or who arrived first in a queue for a popular film. The best way to resolve such a dispute, of course, is by talking it over sensibly and agreeing on the best solution. But people are not always so sensible and they can often let their temper get the better of them. That is when an argument turns more serious, with loud voices and insults sometimes leading to physical fights.

Wider disputes

Larger groups of people, and even countries, can behave in the same way. Like individuals, they often come across areas of disagreement with other groups, and these disagreements can also develop into more serious disputes. Conflicts within countries, such as **civil wars**, **revolutions** and **terrorism**, can be very damaging, and disputes between countries can develop into outright war, with far-reaching effects on those involved.

Developing technology has meant that there are more and more advanced weapons, so wars have become more and more deadly. For centuries people would describe a war as devastating if those killed in it were numbered in thousands. The 20th century, however, introduced warfare on a far greater scale. About 8.5 million soldiers died in the **First World War** (1914–18); in the **Second World War** (1939–45) the number of soldiers killed exceeded 20 million. The total number of deaths have been estimated at between 35 and 60 million.

Many children were forced to fight in the war that tore Liberia apart in the 1990s.

WHAT'S AT ISSUE?

WAR & CONFLICT

Sean Connolly

Heinemann
LIBRARY

www.heinemann.co.uk/library
Visit our website to find out more information about **Heinemann Library** books.

To order:
 Phone 44 (0) 1865 888066
 Send a fax to 44 (0) 1865 314091
🖥 Visit the Heinemann Bookshop at www.hcinemann.co.uk/library to browse our catalogue and order online.

First published in Great Britain by Heinemann Library, Halley Court, Jordan Hill, Oxford OX2 8EJ, a division of Reed Educational and Professional Publishing Ltd. Heinemann is a registered trademark of Reed Educational & Professional Publishing Limited.

OXFORD MELBOURNE AUCKLAND JOHANNESBURG BLANTYRE
GABORONE IBADAN PORTSMOUTH NH (USA) CHICAGO

Designed by Tinstar Design (www.tinstar.co.uk)
Originated by Ambassador Litho Ltd
Printed in Hong Kong/China

ISBN 0 431 03558 X   (hardback)   ISBN 0 431 03566 0   (paperback)
06 05 04 03 02   06 05 04 03 02
10 9 8 7 6 5 4 3 2   10 9 8 7 6 5 4 3 2 1

British Library Cataloguing in Publication Data
Connolly, Sean
    War and Conflict. – (What's at issue?)
    1. International relations – Juvenile literature
    I. Title
    327.1'6

Acknowledgements
The Publishers would like to thank the following for permission to reproduce photographs:
Corbis: pp8, 14, 15, 34, 38, Peter Turnley p5, Dave Bartruff p7, Hulton-Deutsch pp11, 25, 33, Bob Krist p13, AFP pp21, 41x2, Timothy O'Sullivan p23, Bettmann pp24, 27, 37, Paul Seheult p28, Aero Graphics Inc p43; Hulton Getty: p17; Rex Features: pp9, 19, John Gunston p4, Sipa Press p20, Jonathan Banks p30, Andrew Testa p35; Solo Syndication: David Low p31; US Airforce Museum: p36.

Cover photograph: Network: Mike Goldwater.

Our thanks to Julie Turner (Head of Student Services and SENCO, Banbury School, Oxfordshire) for her comments in the preparation of this book.

Every effort has been made to contact copyright holders of any material reproduced in this book. Any omissions will be rectified in subsequent printings if notice is given to the Publisher.

Any words appearing in the text in bold, **like this**, are explained in the Glossary.

An international issue

This book examines the nature of war and conflict, and the results of these international disputes that have got out of control. There are many issues at stake in any discussion of this subject. Just about every new 'advance' in the area of warfare – such as new weapons, larger armies, methods to boost people's spirits and even peacekeeping forces – raises yet more questions about war in general. First it is important to draw a distinction between conflicts and wars.

How this book works

The chapters in this book are grouped so that similar subjects are close together. In this way you will be able to build a clearer picture about war and conflict by understanding how these subjects relate to each other before moving on to another group. The first section talks

International emergency medical staff of the Red Cross treat the wounded in many war zones.

about the history of warfare, from the time of the first civilizations right down to the present day. The next section deals with armies, navies and other armed forces – what they consist of, how they operate and what type of weapons they use. Then there are several chapters on the sort of disputes – or other reasons – that prompt nations to begin wars. Sometimes a war can take place inside just one country. The fourth group of related chapters deals with some very broad issues concerning the way in which wars affect people's ways of thinking. The last section looks at the way that the world tries to prevent future wars, particularly in an age when the most powerful countries have weapons that could destroy the Earth.

The history of war (1)

When **archaeologists** examine the traces of the earliest humans, they usually find weapons. Many of these weapons were used to hunt for food, but it is suspected that even these early humans could turn on each other. The reasons for these disputes, of course, are lost in time but we can assume that hunters would attack anyone that they saw as competing for food or trying to steal supplies. These early battles, perhaps involving only several people, were the first conflicts. Human beings became more advanced, finding better ways to feed and clothe themselves, but conflict remained – and still remains – a part of human life.

A world of progress?

As human society advanced, so too did the methods of fighting. By about 5000 years ago, simple farming communities had developed into advanced civilizations in several parts of the world: in what is now Iraq, in Egypt, in the Indus Valley of India and in China. The people living in these great centres developed systems of writing and **irrigation**; they also produced great buildings. At the same time they began to rely on armies. At first the soldiers' job was simply to defend against people raiding for food. However, more people moved into the cities, and in order to feed them, these cities had to expand. Soldiers who once were simply defenders now had to attack neighbours in order to gain more land for growing food. This expansion led to the great **empires** of Assyria, Persia, India and China.

Survival depended not so much on being the most advanced society, but on being the most powerful military power. New weapons and ways of fighting showed the way forward. Alexander the Great, beginning in what is now Greece, took his army eastward in 334 BC. He defeated the Persians and continued eastward to India, where he defeated the Indian king in 326 BC.

The Romans were becoming a force at about this time. They saw that Alexander had stretched himself too far and could never rule the lands he conquered. So they set about doing the same thing – building an empire – but made sure that each conquered nation remained firmly under Roman rule. Using this method, the Romans developed an empire that stretched from Britain in the west to Egypt in the east. And although the Romans had an advanced society, their success depended on their ability to fight – and win.

Walling off enemies

Many societies that had grown into powerful empires believed that the people outside their boundaries were savages or '**barbarians**'. The Romans lost many of their finest soldiers trying to conquer the people living in what is now Germany. After several such defeats, they decided to push no further and to defend the edge of their empire. They built a series of outposts and forts to guard against attack from these fierce people. In the end, though, these defences were not enough and the barbarians were able to conquer Rome itself in AD 476.

At about the same time a great empire was developing in China. Like the Romans, the Chinese believed that their neighbours were primitive savages. In order to protect themselves from these people they built the Great Wall of China, beginning more than 2500 years ago. This immense structure grew over many centuries and eventually stretched 6700 km (4160 miles) across the Chinese frontier.

Soldiers used to patrol the Great Wall of China while sentries and archers could peer through gaps. Nowadays the wall is a great tourist attraction.

The history of war (2)

Despite great advances in science, medicine and technology in the fifteen centuries between the fall of the Roman **Empire** (in AD 476) to the present, war and conflict have continued throughout. In many cases, the great wars of this period have been fought because of ideas – religion, the notion of a unifying leader or a type of political thinking. If anything, these wars have been fiercer than the 'simpler' wars that were fought to defend or expand national boundaries.

A higher calling

By the **Middle Ages**, Europe was no longer held together by a single powerful empire or its fearsome army. Many Europeans longed for something that would unite the warring nations. They found it in a series of 'holy wars' – the Crusades. The target of these wars was the Arabs, who controlled the Holy Lands, the area where the events in the Bible had taken place. The Arabs were **Muslims**, followers of a religion known as **Islam**. Although the Arabs treated Christian visitors to the Holy Land well, Europeans were horrified that such a sacred place should be ruled by a people they considered their enemy. Beginning in AD 1095, European rulers – who would normally be at war with each other – launched a series of wars called the Crusades to defeat the Arabs. Over nearly 200 years they mounted nine Crusades, causing great damage and bloodshed. In the end, very little was accomplished apart from creating a sense of distrust that would last long after the end of the last Crusade in 1272.

Saladin, one of the main Arab leaders during the Crusades, earned the respect of his Christian enemies.

The lure of strong leaders

Even when a country is at peace, its people are often dissatisfied. They believe that their country would be richer, and life easier, if they had a strong ruler. Sometimes the rate of change in life, with new ways of working and living, strengthens this longing for a world of certainty. At such times strong leaders can take power, convincing their people that military success is the answer to their problems. Napoleon Bonaparte rose to power in France just a decade after the French **Revolution** had changed the country completely in 1789. He set out on a series of wars that at first were aimed simply at defending France. Within years, though, France itself controlled nearly all of Europe.

Adolph Hitler tried to match Napoleon. Hitler achieved power in 20th-century Germany because Germany had become very weak after the **First World War**. Many Germans believed that Hitler was someone who could offer their country strong leadership and hope. But Hitler's way of strengthening Germany involved crushing its neighbours. Hitler's behaviour triggered the **Second World War**, which cost the lives of millions of people around the world.

Do you think leading a country to war is a good way to show strength? In what other ways can strength be shown?

May Day parades in the former Soviet Union inspired the people to be ready for battle in the Cold War.

THE COLD WAR

The two **superpowers** in the middle of the 20th century were the USA and the Soviet Union. They had very different types of governments – a **free market** system in the USA and a **communist** system in the Soviet Union – which led to rivalry and eventually to hostility between them. They also had armies and weapons that could destroy each other and the entire world many times over.

Instead of starting a war that could possibly destroy the world, each side tried to influence the balance of power to their own advantage. They would help small countries in their struggle with the rival superpower and they would constantly threaten to use their weapons. This state of affairs, when the world held its breath every time there was a crisis, was known as the **Cold War**. It lasted from 1945 until 1991, when the Soviet Union's communist system fell apart.

Tactics and strategy

Military leaders see their job as securing victory. And although war is a matter of life and death, the way in which it is planned is sometimes like a game. There are two types of thinking behind winning, both in games and in warfare. **Strategy** is the overall plan, deciding on a way to use the pieces (in a board game) or the troops and supplies (of war) in a way that finally achieves victory – or avoids defeat. **Tactics** describe the thinking along the way, making the most of a sudden advantage, having to overcome unexpected obstacles or making the best of a bad position.

High price

In war, tactics and strategy are designed for military success – but that success can come at a price that many people consider to be too high. In 1864, during the American **Civil War** (see pages 22–3), the US Army commander William Tecumseh Sherman captured and burned the city of Atlanta, Georgia, and then marched his troops hundreds of miles to the sea. Along the way they destroyed nearly everything they came across – farms, offices and factories. His tactic was to strike at the heartland of the enemy, making his opponents too fearful and depressed to continue fighting. Many southerners still resent these cruel actions.

Years later Sherman said, 'War is hell'. Did he mean that people should expect such actions in wartime, or was he viewing what he did in a new light? What do you think?

A nagging question

The six years of the **Second World War** cost many millions of lives. Although there were battles in many parts of the world, the main areas of fighting were in Europe. On the Pacific islands, **allied forces**, led by the USA, Australia and New Zealand, began to win some important battles and regain some of the area held by the Japanese. Their overall strategy was to drive the Japanese back to their own country and then to attack Japan itself, making Japan surrender.

In order to carry out this strategy the **Allies** adopted two very different tactics – one was familiar, but the second one changed the face of history. The first tactic was known as 'island hopping'. It meant that they would defeat the Japanese using air, land and sea power, taking one Japanese-held island at a time. This tactic succeeded, but it was slow and costly. By 1945 the Allies had moved close enough to launch air raids on Japan itself. Up to that point there had been no fighting in Japan, but now those people living in Tokyo, Yokohama and other major Japanese cities were becoming accustomed to hearing air raid warning sirens and the sounds of buildings and bridges being destroyed by bombs. The Allied commanders believed that Japanese **morale** would weaken because of the bombing raids, but the Japanese government showed no sign that it was willing to consider surrender. Public announcements called on the Japanese people to defend their country with all their will. The Allies faced a difficult choice: either continue the dangerous bombing raids – possibly for years – in the hope that they might force a surrender, or to try something altogether more dramatic. That was when the USA moved to its second tactic – using **atomic weapons**.

On 6 August 1945 the USA dropped an atomic bomb on the Japanese city of Hiroshima, and three days later dropped a similar bomb on Nagasaki. The two bombs killed more than 100,000 people, permanently injured thousands more and nearly flattened both cities. The effect was immediate – Japan surrendered on 14 August. At the time, most Americans believed that the bombs saved more lives than they destroyed, by ending the war so quickly. But since then many people have argued that by using these weapons, the USA had begun a process that could destroy the world in a future war.

Do you think that the USA was right to use atomic weapons in 1945? Was it right to drop a second bomb?

German and British soldiers returning from the Battle of the Somme, a First World War battle that saw both sides using the strategy of massing thousands of soldiers against each other.

Armed forces

It is a fact of life that nearly every country has a standing army – a permanent military force that is prepared to defend the nation in case of attack. The earliest civilizations, dating back more than 5000 years, have seen the need to have a constant supply of soldiers ready to attack or defend.

Apart from the risk that having so many armies presents – it increases the chances of war because neighbours often feel threatened – there is another issue at stake. Even many of the smallest countries in the world have such armies, and for the poorest nations this represents an enormous cost. Very often these countries feel that they must keep their armed forces supplied with food and money because there is always the chance that the military might crush the government. Doing this means that the neediest people go without important supplies and the country remains in a state of constant poverty.

FACT

Countries with largest armed forces:*
- *China 2,930,000*
- *USA 1,547,000*
- *Russia 1,520,000*
- *India 1,145,000*
- *North Korea 1,125,000*
- *South Korea 663,000*
- *Pakistan 587,000*
- *Vietnam 572,000*
- *Iran 513,000*
- *Turkey 507,800*

* figures are the total number of personnel working in all services

Should women fight?

Traditionally going off to war was a 'man's job'. People generally believed that women were too weak – and possibly too peaceful – to become good soldiers. The great armies of the past, from the **First World War**, to those involved in the Crusades of the **Middle Ages**, were all male.

By the middle of the 20th century this picture had begun to change. Women had pressed for equal rights in many countries, and one of these rights was to serve in the armed forces. Up until the **Second World War** women could join many armies – such as those of Britain, Australia and the USA – but they could not actually fight. Since the war, most countries have accepted women in virtually all military roles.

PLANNING FOR PEACE

The countries of Central America have had a history of warfare, which has included conflicts between countries and **rebellions** within some of the countries. As a result, keeping a standing army has become an important feature of countries in the region. There is one exception, which many small countries around the world see as a possible example. Costa Rica got rid of its army in 1948 in a move that showed how confident it was that conflicts within the country – and with its neighbours – could be resolved peacefully. Since then, Costa Rica has remained peaceful and – perhaps as a result – richer than its neighbours. The losing parties in elections accept defeat and hope to gain power next time by persuading the people rather than threatening them with force.

A female cadet about to become an officer, at West Point, the US military academy.

Branching out

Modern armed forces fall into several different categories, or branches. Armies remain important as they have for more than 5000 years, although their equipment is now very advanced. The other traditional branch of the military, the navy, is as vital for coastal countries as it has been for hundreds of years. In addition, there is the air force, with planes, helicopters and other aircraft ready to be used in battle. Backing up all these branches is the intelligence service, whose job it is to gather information about the size and power of possible enemies.

By the end of the 20th century the overall number of people making the different branches of the armed forces – at least among the most powerful nations – had declined. Fewer people were needed to fight, it was believed, because the end of the **Cold War** in the 1990s had lessened the risk of a major world conflict. The prospect of a third world war, once a very real possibility, became less worrying to most governments. However, the threat of **terrorism** and regional conflicts has meant that governments still spend enormous sums on keeping their armed forces up to date.

Armed forces, like computers or other equipment, need to be modern in order to keep up with the rest of the world. As a result, trillions of dollars are spent on warfare – money that could be used to build peace and prosperity.

Weapons of war

A country that is at war is always trying to find an advantage over its enemy in order to secure victory. There are obvious advantages, such as having a larger army or a better understanding of the landscape where battles might be fought. But one of the most important advantages that any warring nation can hold is an advantage in weapons.

Humans have used science and technology to construct more effective weapons throughout history. Evidence dating back to the first humans indicates that many of these developments – such as the first use of arrows, spear and slings – were needed in order to hunt large animals. But **archaeologists** have found that some human bones from that period have the same wound marks as those of deer and bears. The same new weapons had been used to settle conflicts among these early people. It stands to reason that the first group to develop any of these weapons would be able to defeat a rival group – the same is true today.

Action and reaction

There are many examples in history where ownership of better weaponry has brought victory. The English army defeated the French at the Battle of Crécy in 1346 because their men had longbows, which could shoot arrows further than the bow used by the French. Likewise, the introduction of the crossbow and gunpowder at about the same time gave some armies a real advantage.

The Gatling gun, designed in the mid-19th century, was a forerunner of the modern machine gun.

But almost as soon as a new weapon has been introduced, people have tried to find ways of limiting its use. The **feudal** societies of medieval Europe and Japan had laws and customs to keep such weapons in the hands of noblemen, so that wars would not spread widely. In those days Europeans looked to the Roman Catholic Church to limit both new weapons and the scale of warfare. In 1139 the Second Lateran Council, called by the Roman Catholic Church, banned the use of the crossbow against Christians, although not against those the church considered **infidels**. Similar agreements tried to limit the use of other weapons and types of warfare.

14

The 'Star Wars' debate

The issue of new weapons remains important today. During the **Cold War** the USA and the Soviet Union spent vast amounts of money building new **atomic weapons**, aimed mainly at each other. This competition was called the Arms Race. Despite the construction of all these weapons, most people believed, and certainly hoped, that they would never be used. In a sense, there was a balance because each side feared that the other would respond to any attack with similar weapons.

Then, in March 1983, US President Ronald Reagan announced plans for a new weapons system, the Strategic Defense Initiative (SDI). Using this system, the USA would have sensors and lasers orbiting the Earth, and launch weapons as necessary, so that any missiles on their way to the USA would be **intercepted** and destroyed. Because it involved battles in space, the SDI was soon nicknamed the 'Star Wars' system.

Many scientists believed that it would not work, but there were other objections, mainly from the Soviet side. These objectors argued that the decades-old 'balance' would be destroyed, allowing the USA to attack the Soviet Union without fear of their attacking back. The debate raged for several years, but the project was put aside when the Soviet Union split into its member countries in 1991. Less expensive systems have been proposed since then, but the issue remains whether they are simply defensive, as claimed, or whether they really act as a shield for launching attacks.

US President Ronald Reagan chose a nationwide television broadcast to announce the 'Star Wars' system in 1983.

Conquest and empires

There is an old saying that 'might makes right'. It means that, in a sense, strength is the deciding factor in a contest, and by winning you are in a position to believe your **cause** is right and the loser's is wrong. Over the course of history, there have been many examples of countries that grow and become powerful, and then set about conquering their neighbours. They believed their might gave them that right. Unless they met an equally powerful enemy, such nations kept on gaining territory, which they ruled as an **empire**. Good examples include ancient China and Rome about 2000 years ago, the Ottoman Empire of Turkey about 650 years ago and Napoleon's France.

Very often the imperial rulers believe that far from crushing the different nations that make up the empire, they are offering the people the chance to become part of a more efficient, powerful grouping. In addition, the new rulers often build new roads, bridges and government buildings. The new construction, of course, helps the empire by allowing armies to travel through more easily, but throughout history local inhabitants have benefited from some aspects of imperial rule: from Roman courts of law, French trading routes and the British style of government, for example. However, it is just as easy for the conquered nations to feel like second-class citizens whose hard work ultimately benefits only the 'mother country'. When this type of thinking spreads throughout the population as a whole the time becomes right for **rebellion** and **revolution** (see pages 24–25).

When empires meet

Several European countries conquered large parts of the Americas in the 16th and 17th centuries. The Spanish, however, had to defeat two mighty empires in order to gain control of Central and South America. Like the British and French in North America, they believed that they were bringing civilization to 'savages' – the Native Americans living there. However, their wars of conquest crushed the thriving cultures of the Aztec Empire in Mexico and the Inca Empire in the Andes of South America, absorbing what they found useful into the Spanish Empire. The Spanish benefited greatly, gaining gold and silver mines, thousands of people to work for them and even a collection of ready-made cities. The Aztecs and Incas, and their descendants, lost all control of the lands they once ruled.

The British had a slightly different experience in India during the 18th century. The Mughal Empire, which had ruled much of India for centuries, had just been broken up, and the British were able to gain power relatively easily. Their military superiority ensured that most of India became the 'jewel in the crown' of the British Empire. The British provided new roads, schools and systems of government, but they were quick to use force to fight back any Indian moves for independence.

The 'Scramble for Africa'

By the middle of the 19th century several European countries – notably the UK,

France, Germany and the Netherlands – had powerful economies. They had benefited from the **Industrial Revolution** and were keen to find new places where they could sell goods. They also needed to find sources of cheap raw materials, such as cotton, oil and timber, to keep their factories thriving. With these aims in mind, these countries sought to build or develop empires by setting up **colonies** in Asia and, more commonly, Africa.

Several of these powerful European nations competed and sometimes fought with each other as they set out to claim African territories for themselves. This competition became known as the 'Scramble for Africa'. After a series of small wars, conflicts and treaties, much of Africa was in the hands of one or other of these countries by the end of the century.

The leaders and senior military officials of three European empires – Germany, Austria-Hungary and Russia – met in 1872 to agree on ways to co-operate. Other contact between European powers led to rivalry and warfare.

The one group that was not consulted in the process of agreeing who controlled which area was the African people themselves. Borders drawn by Europeans divided many existing African nations; some African nations found themselves grouped with other Africans of a different culture or religion – and sometimes traditional enemies were forced together within European colonies. This unnatural division of the continent led to many conflicts in the 20th century, when the colonies began to gain their independence (see pages 18–19).

Ethnic conflicts

Throughout history, several types of dispute have traditionally flared up into outright war. One of the most violent of these has been between **ethnic** groups. Sometimes their differences are linked to religion (see pages 20–21), but just as often they boil down to the way in which each group identifies itself. In Europe and elsewhere since the Middle Ages, many large countries have broken up into smaller nations. Sometimes these newly independent nations have become part of a larger, and supposedly united, country or **empire**. In modern times these larger groupings have broken down and newly independent nations have returned to their age-old conflicts.

> ### FACT
>
> *Ethnic make-up in*
> *Yugoslavia (before break-up):*
> - *36% Serbs*
> - *20% Croats*
> - *9% Muslims*
> - *8% Slovenes*
> - *6% Macedonians*
> - *6% Albanians*
> - *15% others*

Melting pots that boil over

Some countries contain only one major ethnic group. The people within the group feel that they have a shared history, culture, language and outlook on life in general. For example, most of the people living in Norway see themselves as Norwegian; likewise more than 90 per cent of Slovenians belong to the same ethnic group. Other countries are more complicated and have many different groups represented in their population. The USA has historically welcomed new people; their differences would become less important as they joined the American 'melting pot'. On the whole this has worked, and most Americans – from whatever original background – now see themselves as Americans.

Other countries are less lucky. Sometimes a nation is conquered by a powerful neighbour and it can no longer maintain its traditions freely. This occurred when China conquered Tibet in 1951. Nowadays, Tibetans cannot practise much of their traditional religion in their own land, and Tibetan exiles are asking other countries to press China to allow Tibet its freedom. Then there are countries which have different ethnic groups within their borders, but which – unlike the USA – cannot prevent violence between them. The eastern European country of Yugoslavia split up in the early 1990s because of such disputes, and there was terrible fighting there for almost a decade, as different ethnic groups fought each other.

Can you think of any countries where different ethnic groups live together in peace? Why don't they turn against each other?

> ### FACT
>
> *Ethnic make-up in Rwanda and Burundi:*
> - *85% Hutu*
> - *14% Tutsi*
> - *1% Twa pygmy*

THE AFRICAN NIGHTMARE

Africa, much of which had been carved up by European powers in the 19th century (see pages 16–17), was also the scene of terrible fighting at the end of the 20th century and into the 21st. One of the worst cases was that of Rwanda and its neighbour, Burundi. There are two main ethnic groups in these countries, the Tutsi and the Hutu. Ruled as one country under Germany, and then Belgium, they became independent in 1962. In Burundi there was a degree of harmony between the two groups, but in Rwanda there were many clashes from the 1960s onwards. These became far more violent in the 1990s after Rwanda's president was killed; his plane was shot down and both ethnic groups blamed each other. Violence turned to outright conflict – thousands were killed and many more were forced to flee the country. Each side committed horrific acts of violence, and sometimes the **refugees** from the war were afraid to return because they feared revenge from the other group. Even a **United Nations** peacekeeping force (see pages 40–41) failed to stop the bloodshed and the violence has continued. Some figures suggest that Rwanda lost more than a quarter of its original population – those who had either been killed or fled to other countries.

These protesters in London support the call for Tibet's independence rather than its present position as part of China. Senior Chinese officials meet similar protests around the world.

Religious divides

Nearly every religion in the world tries to teach its believers to accept their neighbours and to work for peaceful solutions to problems. However, because each religion is slightly different from others, people often believe that theirs is better. That belief leads some groups of people, even countries, to wage war with each other. Sometimes the wars occur because one group will not allow another religious group to worship freely. At other times the war is almost a war of conquest, trying to force another group to change their way of belief. And then there are conflicts that seem to be religious, because the two sides have different religious beliefs, but are really about other matters.

In the name of God?

Many governments nowadays ensure that all their citizens enjoy freedom of speech, freedom of action and freedom of religion (including the right to have no religion at all). Unfortunately, this **tolerant** approach has not always been common and even now people suffer – and fight – for their beliefs.

The European Crusades of the Middle Ages (see pages 8–9) are good examples of religious wars. The Christians of Europe believed that **Muslims** in the Holy Lands were **infidels**. It was only this shared hatred that united many Europeans, and they believed that their wars were fought 'in the name of God'. If they had bothered to look more closely they would have seen that the Muslim nations were far more tolerant, offering Christians and

These Hizbollah fighters in Lebanon believe that their actions are in keeping with the highest ideals of Islam.

Jews freedom and important jobs within the government. But the need to go to war, and the sense of belonging that it developed, made Europeans want to believe that the Muslims were evil – and almost less than human.

The idea of a 'holy war' is still alive today, although now it is more common among Muslims. Some Muslims believe that the actions of some governments, including their own, are opposed to **Islam**. In their view, it is right, and even holy, to try to destroy these governments, even through the use of **terrorism**.

A wrong title

Other conflicts are often described as religious wars but in reality are more complicated. The Thirty Years War, fought between Catholic and Protestant regions of Europe in the 17th century, is often given this description. But although each side hated the other's religion, the war really dragged on because it came at a time when new nations were taking the place of older nations. The different religion that each side chose to follow became an easy way of identifing them.

There are similar, more recent conflicts. The long-running conflict in Northern Ireland, for example, also involves Catholics and Protestants. But neither side is trying to change the other's beliefs. Instead, the religious labels identify two ethnic groups – those who identify with the Irish in the Irish Republic (largely Catholic) and those who feel themselves to be British (mainly Protestant). The terrible wars in the former Yugoslavia during the 1990s also had a religious element. Catholics, Orthodox Christians and Muslims fought each other – not in the name of their religion but really in a fierce dispute about land ownership.

ANTI-RELIGIOUS STATE

The **communist ideology** of the Soviet Union (which existed between 1917 and 1991) was anti-religious. The government believed that religion was foolish, and religious belief among the population was actively discouraged. It imprisoned religious leaders and closed most of the places of worship. These included not only the churches of the Russian Orthodox believers (Russia's largest religious group), but also Catholic and Protestant churches, Jewish synagogues, Islamic mosques and Buddhist temples. In Saint Petersburg, one of Russia's largest cities, a 'Museum of the History of Religion and **Atheism**' was set up to try and show the Soviet people that religion only divides people and makes them warlike. The museum showed scenes of religious wars through the centuries, but ignored the sense of peace that many believers feel because of their religion.

Many Protestants in Northern Ireland march each year to commemorate old victories over Catholics.

Civil wars

Just as you learn about more and more difficult ideas as you go through school, so, too, do nations – at least this is what many people hope. We look back proudly through history to find ideas that have led to progress and better lives. Development of scientific ideas has brought us modern industry, health systems and even entertainment. Unfortunately, ideas that lie behind how we govern ourselves have not always been so successful. They can cause serious disputes, to the point that a country will tear itself apart in a **civil war**. The people might still feel united as an ethnic group, and have no religious quarrels, but the war develops over the basic principles about running the country itself.

Sometimes the dispute echoes a wider conflict. Many countries in the 20th century had civil wars that pitted **communist** thinkers against those who believed that individuals should have more say in how a country is ruled. This was the same issue that divided the USA and the Soviet Union during the **Cold War** (see pages 8–9), although those two **superpowers** never actually fought each other.

The right to rule

Modern ideas about how a country should be governed developed in the 16th and 17th centuries. New nations were becoming more powerful, and the issue of who exactly should have the power to rule over them became increasingly important. Matters came to a head in England in the 1640s. The English king, Charles I, believed that he had a 'divine right' to rule over the English people. In other words, he and his supporters believed that God wanted a strong king to have power. Others believed that the people themselves should have a greater say, through their elected representatives in **Parliament**.

The dispute turned into outright war – the English Civil War. The people of England took sides and the armies of the king and of Parliament fought a number of bloody battles. Eventually Parliament won, and Charles was put to death. Parliament took power, but only for about ten years. After that time the English chose to have a monarch (king or queen) again, but the effects of Parliament's earlier victory still showed. Today, England still has a monarchy, but the monarch has much less power than Parliament.

America divided

From its earliest days the USA found it hard to resolve a fundamental question about its structure – how much power each state should have and how much should rest with the national government. Many of the southern states believed that states should be able to make most of their own laws, free from central control. They had an additional reason to take this view. Southern farmers owned many African-American slaves who worked on their huge cotton and tobacco farms. Northerners did not approve of slavery and tried to end the practice throughout the country.

In 1861, eleven southern states **seceded** from the United States of America in order to form their own country. Their new country, the Confederate States of America, would preserve the power of individual states, including the right to own slaves. The 23 remaining states, mostly in the north, believed that this action would destroy the United States, and so took up arms against the new country. What followed was a civil war in every sense of the word. Families, particularly those living along the border states between the north and the south, often had sons fighting on either side. Apart from the slavery issue, which was enough in itself to inspire many northerners to take up arms, the basic principle lay in the choice between loyalty to one's state or to one's country. General Robert E. Lee, who had been the country's most admired soldier before the war, was offered the command of either the United States (northern) army or that of the Confederate army. He eventually chose loyalty to his home state, Virginia, and led the Confederate forces throughout the war. He had the painful duty of sending his troops to fight against his former comrades. The Civil War lasted four years and took a terrible toll on both sides, especially the south. In the end, the south was defeated and the United States of America was once more one country. And with the US victory came new laws that freed the slaves in every US state.

The US Civil War had many casualties, from the thousands of men who died to the bitter memories that lingered for decades.

Rebellion and revolution

Civil war is not the only type of major conflict that occurs within a country. Sometimes a large group of people, even the **majority** of the population, can trigger a clash with government forces that develops into a fierce struggle. This in turn can grow strong enough to topple the government itself. One thing these struggles have in common is that at the beginning it usually seems as though the ruling power is too powerful to question, sometimes using force to scare people into obeying its rules. So, why would people abandon their daily routines, and their way of earning a living, in order to risk their lives in a struggle against such a powerful opponent?

Popular uprisings

There are many reasons to explain these disputes, but in general they fall into one of two categories. The first is usually called a revolt or a **rebellion**. This type of conflict often has its roots in a sense of **ethnic** identity among most of the people in a country. Usually the country is ruled by a group that represents a different ethnic group. For example, in the 16th century, Spain ruled the lands that are now the Netherlands in northern Europe. The rulers of what was called the Spanish

Netherlands spoke a different language and followed a different religion from the people that they ruled. The Dutch people mounted a series of rebellions which eventually led to their independence in 1648.

South Africa had a different experience, but it also amounted to a rebellion. Since the 17th century the descendants of white Europeans held power in South Africa, although most people there are black Africans. This white rule became known as **apartheid** in 1948, and many laws made it difficult for non-whites to own land, vote or work where they chose. Black South Africans and their supporters held many protests, and were sometimes

Bangladeshi soldiers display captured weapons during their successful rebellion against Pakistan in 1971.

killed by the police, in their efforts to change the government. Meanwhile, the world began to learn more about the conditions in South Africa, and there were many international efforts to promote change in the country. So, although the anti-apartheid movement began as a weak force, it gained many powerful allies who could help force the hand of the white South African government. Apartheid was eventually ended in the late 1980s and free elections were held in 1994.

Will of the people?

Other rebellions are called **revolutions**. These are also led – at least at first – by a small group who represent the majority of the people in a nation. The rulers are not foreigners, but they deny the people many freedoms and rights. The French people overthrew their king in 1789 in the French Revolution. The new government tried to change society by guaranteeing many rights to the people. In the same way, the Russian people overthrew their tsar (a king or emperor) in 1917. The Russian Revolution replaced royal government with a **communist** system, which survived for 74 years before it, too, was replaced in 1991. Both of these revolutions inspired people in other countries to overthrow governments that many people believed treated their citizens unfairly. China followed Russia's example in 1949, setting up a communist system that is still in place today.

CHINESE UPRISING

China's rulers are aware of the power of 'the will of the people'. That is how they gained power, but they also know that it is how they might lose it. On 4 June 1989 thousands of Chinese people marched to Tiananmen Square in the capital, Beijing. They demanded changes and more freedom from the government. The government sent in troops to end the protest and hundreds of the protesters were killed.

China paid a price for its powerful crushing of the Tiananmen Square protests. It was denied important trading deals, and international efforts put pressure on the Chinese government to free many of the imprisoned Tiananmen Square protesters.

Vladimir Lenin, here addressing a crowd, was the leader of the revolution that overthrew Russia's Tsar in 1917.

Guerrilla warfare

At first glance, it seems hard to imagine how any **rebellion** or **revolution** could succeed. After all, the ruling power – whether a foreign-controlled government or simply a strong national system – seems to have all the advantages. It has the wealth, the trained army and all the best equipment. Its opponents, even if they represent a **majority** of the people, have only numbers on their side. The secret to success lies in **tactics** and **strategy**.

The strategy in most rebellions is eventually to gain overall control of a country by defeating the more powerful opponent. This victory usually comes about when the opponent loses their will to fight – their **morale** is broken. The way in which this victory is secured – the tactics – often depends on **guerrilla** warfare. Guerrilla is the Spanish word for 'little war', and it is a good description of a conflict that has very few big battles but many small **skirmishes**. The rebels use their knowledge of the countryside – and the support of the people who live there – to make sudden, unexpected attacks and then to vanish into forests or hills. A larger army, caught off-guard, cannot react quickly enough to chase and eliminate the small band of rebels. Over the course of time this type of warfare can wear down the powerful army, so that its troops become constantly afraid and even unwilling to fight.

The word 'guerrilla' was invented to describe the resistance of the Spanish people to the powerful French armies led by Napoleon Bonaparte in the early 19th century. They would attack French camps at night, kill a handful of soldiers and then disappear into the darkness. Those French soldiers who survived – even though they outnumbered their enemy – would worry each night about similar Spanish raids. As a result they became less willing to remain in Spain to continue fighting. Many South American countries used a similar strategy to gain their independence from Spain soon after that period.

A taste of things to come

The USA has been linked to guerrilla wars twice in its history. It gained its independence through such tactics. American colonists in the 1770s and 1780s grouped together in small bands of 'minutemen' – ordinary farmers and townspeople who were prepared to fight the British at a minute's notice. They won a number of important skirmishes against the more powerful British army, and over the course of seven years made it almost impossible for the British to continue fighting. Two centuries later, however, the US government ignored the lesson of their history and suffered a major defeat from just such an approach in Vietnam.

A superpower defeated

Vietnam had been a French **colony** for many years, but faced a long and bitter rebellion staged by the Vietnamese who wanted independence. The rebellion was led by a group from North Vietnam called the Viet Minh, who wanted to form a **communist** government in Vietnam.

The Viet Minh gained control of the northern part of the country in 1945 but wanted to unite the country under their rule. They succeeded in driving the French out in 1954 and seven years later began trying to defeat the anti-communist south.

The USA sent several hundred troops to help South Vietnam in 1961. Over the next few years many more US soldiers arrived – by 1968 there were 525,000 Americans fighting in Vietnam. The Americans had modern rifles, mortars and cannons, backed up by modern aircraft and ships offshore. The Viet Minh, who had now joined with the Viet Cong, had very little equipment and travelled around by bicycle or through secret tunnels in the jungle. They could appear and disappear in a flash, which made it almost impossible for the Americans to defeat them. Over the years, American morale

FACTS

It is estimated that the following people were killed during the Vietnam War:
- *1 million North Vietnamese soldiers*
- *1 million Vietnamese **civilians***
- *200,000 South Vietnamese soldiers*
- *56,555 US soldiers.*

The Vietnam War also destroyed:
- *50% of the country's forest cover*
- *25 million acres of its agricultural land.*

weakened and public demand for an end to US involvement in Vietnam steadily grew. The US government began to slowly pull out of the conflict from about 1969 onwards, but by 1975 the North Vietnamese troops had captured all of the country. The guerrilla tactics had secured a victory against the most powerful nation in the world.

Viet Cong guerrillas hid weapons and travelled through a network of tunnels nicknamed the 'Ho Chi Minh Trail' in honour of their leader.

Terrorism

Terrorism, as its name suggests, involves using fear as a weapon. It can involve planting bombs in public places, kidnapping famous people or threatening to use terrible weapons if certain demands are not met. In each case, the terrorists hope that the public will be so terrified by the possibility of death and violence that they will force the government to give in on a particular issue. In this respect, terrorism is a **tactic** that is similar to **guerrilla** warfare. In each case, fear is used to destroy the **morale** of the opponent.

There is sometimes support shown by one terrorist faction for another, as this painting in Northern Ireland shows.

Right or wrong?

The groups that use terrorism are usually small compared with what they consider to be their enemy. They might be a group seeking independence from a larger nation, people who disagree with the religious policies of a government, or simply people who want no government at all. Although the wider world may agree with the terrorist's **cause**, or at least understand it, their methods rarely win them support. In fact, most people are repelled by what terrorists do. But does terrorism work?

Two groups that have long been linked to terrorism are the Palestine Liberation

Organization (PLO) and the Irish Republican Army (IRA). The PLO demand a guarantee of land for the Palestinian people in the Middle East; the IRA is fighting for a different system of government in Ireland. In each case the cause supported by the organization seems reasonable enough. But both groups have been involved in kidnappings, bombings and the murder of innocent people, always as a way of gaining publicity for their cause. And in recent years, both groups have seen some of their demands met, after lengthy **negotiations**. The world breathed a sigh of relief when it seemed that their use of terrorism had ended. But many within these groups believe that they only achieved what they did *because* they used terrorism. And if they believe this to be true, then others around the world might do so also.

Changing reputations

One of the most difficult issues surrounding terrorism centres on what happens when a group that has a reputation for terrorism succeeds in its aims. In South Africa, for example, black people – who make up most of the population – had been denied many rights under the **apartheid** system of the white government. They set up the African National Congress (ANC) as a way of pressing for equality.

For decades, their peaceful protests had no effect – and many blacks were killed by the army or police. Then, in 1960, the South African police killed 69 black protesters in a town called Sharpeville. As a result, a year later the ANC decided to use violent methods if necessary to force changes in South Africa. The ANC leader,

Nelson Mandela, formed a secret ANC army that attacked government buildings and communications systems. Mandela was sentenced to life imprisonment in 1964. Many governments, including those of the USA, took the view that the ANC was a terrorist organization and that Mandela was himself a terrorist.

Gradually, though, the world began to see that Mandela and the ANC had been fighting for a genuine cause, and that the South African government had been **undemocratic**. Many in South Africa itself came to see this, and in 1990 Mandela was released. Within four years apartheid was scrapped and Mandela was elected president. The same governments that had once considered Mandela to be a terrorist now hailed him as a hero.

The case of Mandela was clear-cut. Few would disagree that his cause was just and that he genuinely wanted peace. But what of the dozens of other leaders who are now branded as terrorists?

> ### FACTS
>
> *South Africa, since its free elections, has been described as a 'Rainbow nation'. The ANC's aims, during its struggle against apartheid, had been to ensure equal status for all the different groups in South Africa. These groups comprised:*
> - *76.1% black*
> - *12.8 % white*
> - *8.5% coloured (people of African and white heritage)*
> - *2.6% Asians*
>
> *The blacks belong to nine ethnic groups: Zulu, Xhosa, Pedi, Sotho, Tswana, Tsonga, Swazi, Ndebele and Venda.*

All in the mind?

Morale is an important factor in all wars. Soldiers must feel that they are fighting for a just **cause**, and moreover, that they have a chance to win. They also need to feel they have the support of the general public. Many people in the USA, for example, began to feel that their country should not be fighting in Vietnam (see pages 26–7), even though the war was popular at the beginning. The eventual US withdrawal from Vietnam – amounting to a defeat – came about partly because of this loss of morale.

Leading by example

Most governments realize the importance of morale, especially when things seem to be going badly during a war. The British Prime Minister Winston Churchill, for example, made many speeches and appeared in bombed-out London ruins when Britain was suffering from German bombings during the **Second World War**. That type of action was good leadership, and it could hardly be criticized. Other successful wartime leaders, including Mao Zedong of China and Franklin Roosevelt of the USA, used similar methods to build public support.

Misleading the public

These same leaders, however, need to make some difficult decisions which can lead them to trample on liberties that people normally take for granted. They often use **propaganda** to give a misleading picture of success on the battlefield. Freedom of the press, which

Large signs and billboards dominate the landscape of Cuba, warning Cubans that the US is evil.

The British mocked both the Germans and Russians during the Second World War.

took on powers that the US **Constitution** sets aside for other members of government. He expanded the army, blockaded southern ports and had opponents of the war jailed without trial. Lincoln argued that he needed to make quick decisions, and to appear strong, if his soldiers were to win. With his stronger powers, and the powerful image he produced, Lincoln achieved his victory – but US historians still cannot agree on whether he did the right thing.

normally allows newspapers to print what they like, is strictly controlled. The government also looks carefully at films and plays, giving full support to those that 'help the cause'.

Wartime measures can go even further, sometimes threatening the very liberties that a country believes it is protecting. During the US Civil War (see pages 22–3), for example, President Abraham Lincoln

What do you think? Is it right for wartime leaders to mislead the public into thinking that things are better than they are?

BRAINWASHING

The science of psychology, or the study of the human mind, has led to several unpleasant developments in the way wars are fought. Chief among these is the notion of 'brainwashing' – deliberately controlling a person's mind so that they think in a different way. Over the years it has become common to question prisoners of war about the strength and position of their own army. There are many international rules and regulations that are meant to ensure that such questioning is done fairly. But some governments have been accused of using drugs or cruel treatment to make a prisoner's mind 'snap'. So, even if the

prisoner has given up no information, they become something of a weapon when released – turning weapons on their own army, for example, or leading soldiers into an enemy **ambush**.

Brainwashing is very difficult to prove, and even the accusation is a type of propaganda. It suggests that the enemy is less than human and – if there is no proof – misleads soldiers and the general public. The USA, for example, accused Chinese and north Korean soldiers of brainwashing captured US soldiers during the Korean War of 1950–53. The Chinese and Koreans continue to deny the charge.

Genocide

Some early warrior-armies, such as the forces commanded by Alexander the Great in the 4th century BC and by the Mongol Genghis Khan in the 13th century AD, were able to sweep through enemy countries at great speed. They could defeat other armies quickly on the battlefield and sometimes destroy their cities while they pressed on to further battles. But they never had the power to wipe out an entire country – killing every member of an **ethnic** group or nation.

Modern warfare has made such a wide-scale killing – known as **genocide** – possible. Quite apart from nuclear weapons, which so far have only been used twice in Japan in 1945 (see page 10–11), there is a whole range of arms that can turn this nightmare into a possibility. And several tragic episodes of the 20th century indicate that there are leaders who would be prepared to take such action, if it were in their power.

The power of hatred

A bitter hatred of the enemy often lies at the heart of countries that are at war. **Propaganda**, which is not a new idea, feeds this view while it builds up support for the **cause** of war. Over the centuries, at one time or another, countries have been accused of burning or spearing babies, setting fire to houses full of people and tearing the tongues out of prisoners. Added to these images is the reason that drives many countries to war in the first place: a sense that an enemy is somehow less than human and therefore deserves to be treated like an animal, or worse.

> ### FACT
>
> *Genocide figures:*
> - *Turkey (1914–18)*
> *1.1–1.8 million Armenians killed or sent to prison camps*
> - *Germany and Poland (1939–45)*
> *5–6 million Jews, 400,000 Gypsies, 200,000–340,000 Serbs killed*
> - *Cambodia (1975)*
> *1.5–2 million people (mainly city dwellers) killed*
> - *Rwanda (1994)*
> *500,000–800,000 Tutsis killed*

Sometimes, however, this 'less than human' group lives within the same country. A cruel leader can turn the public against such a group, making it a **scapegoat** for all the difficulties facing a country. The most extreme and tragic example of this process occurred in Germany during the 1930s and 1940s. Germany had suffered greatly during and after the **First World War**. Its leader in the 1930s was Adolph Hitler, who claimed that Jewish people were the reason for many of Germany's problems. His government began to treat Jewish people harshly, and by the time of the **Second World War** many Jews were being executed. These people, of course, were not to blame at all, but during the course of the 'Final Solution' (Hitler's term for his treatment of the Jewish people), some six million people died. Because many of these innocent people died in special ovens, the tragic episode became known as the Holocaust (from the Greek word for 'entirely burnt').

THE KILLING FIELDS

Hitler's attempt to wipe out the Jewish people is, unfortunately, not the only recent example of genocide. Hitler had tried to show how the Jewish people were foreigners, who had no part in Germany. The case of Cambodia was different – it was aimed directly at the same ethnic group as the leaders. Pol Pot was a **communist** leader who came to power in the Asian country of Cambodia in the 1970s, soon after the end of the Vietnam War (see pages 26–7). Like the Viet Cong leaders, he had relied on 'ordinary people' to achieve his victory. But unlike the victorious Vietnamese, Pol Pot then turned his attention on anyone he considered to be rich, educated or otherwise likely to oppose his government. He forced people out of the cities and into the countryside, to work on farms. Conditions on these farms were so harsh that they became known as the 'killing fields'. In the space of two years between 1.5 and 2 million people died because of starvation, disease or execution.

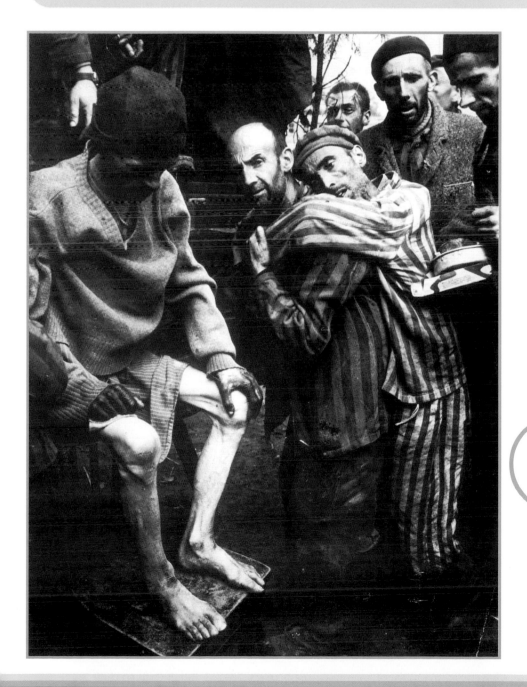

Even the survivors of the concentration camps resembled skeletons when they were freed in 1948. These Jewish prisoners were victims of Hitler's attempts to destroy the Jewish population.

The cost of war

The cost of keeping armed forces is high and always rising. It is a major amount of the total spending in some countries, such as Israel, Iran, Afghanistan and Rwanda. This is not surprising, since all of these countries have recently been involved in major conflicts or feel the need (in the case of Israel) to be constantly prepared against attack from hostile neighbours. But there are also high costs for countries that have had peaceful histories. New Zealand, for example, has friendly relations with all of its neighbours but still spends just under a billion dollars a year on military equipment.

What money cannot buy

More important than the financial cost is the price that people around the world must pay for war itself. Of course, spending increases during times of war, but the effects of a war – even on the winning side – are long-lasting and costly. First, there is the toll of human life. The Soviet Union, for example, lost about 20 million people during the **Second World War**. This number included not just soldiers but **civilians**, and many villages were either destroyed by fighting or were deserted because of all the people who died. The country suffered terribly and for years afterwards it was hard to find enough people to work in some factories or farms. It was hard to imagine that the Soviet Union had been on the winning side. Britain – another winner in that war – also suffered after the war, taking many years to reach the position it might have enjoyed had the war not occurred.

Worthless wallpaper

The position of defeated countries is usually much more grim, and can sometimes set the stage for yet more wars. Germany, defeated in the **First World War**, spent years trying to get

Nazi rallies were a source of pride for many Germans in the 1930s, offering unity and discipline.

Thousands lost their homes during the Kosovo conflict in 1999.

These people need to find somewhere to live and work if they cannot return home. International organizations such as the **Red Cross** and the **United Nations** build temporary camps, but the real problem comes when winter arrives, and it is too cold to live in tents. Many of these **refugees** try to move to the peaceful nations of western Europe and the USA. However, life becomes difficult for them even here. Some of the people in these countries do not believe that the new arrivals are genuine, so they make it hard for them to settle in the new country. In the end, they remain a problem – for their home country, their hoped-for new country, and most tragically for themselves.

back on its feet. Its government in the 1920s could not get people back to work and watched as companies went out of business. Money was almost worthless and people had to fill wheelbarrows with notes just to buy shoes. Some people did not save or spend the money they earned; instead they even used paper money as wallpaper. Those were the conditions that kept the Germans feeling crushed and in need of someone who would lead them out of their difficulties. It was in such a climate that Adolph Hitler came to power, offering a solution to these post-war problems – solutions that led to the Second World War.

Refugees

Millions of people lose their homes because of war. Their villages might be destroyed or they might return after the fighting has ended to find that a new government will not treat them fairly. The wars fought in the former Yugoslavia in the 1990s led to millions of people being forced from their towns and villages because they belonged to the wrong **ethnic** group: this process became known as 'ethnic cleansing'.

FACTS

Of the world's more than 20 million refugees in 2000:
- *6.4 million were living in Southwest Asia (mostly Iran and Pakistan), North Africa and the Middle East*
- *5.5 million in Africa, south of the Sahara*
- *5.4 million in Europe and North America (including 1 million in the USA)*
- *1.5 million in Latin America and the Caribbean*
- *1.2 million in the remaining countries of Asia and Oceania.*

The nuclear element

Nuclear weapons, sometimes called **atomic weapons**, unleash the power of the atom – one of the smallest particles of matter – to create a huge explosion. This power was understood for many years before the **Second World War** but it was only during that war that scientists began to think of using this destructive force to create a weapon. By the middle of the war, scientists in the USA and Germany were engaged in a 'race' to produce the first atomic bomb. Both sides knew that whoever won that race would almost certainly win the war.

The great unknown

Although the scientists knew that such a bomb would be extremely powerful, they could not be sure about just how powerful it would be. Atomic blasts use what is called a chain reaction, meaning that the force of splitting one atom releases energy to open others, which in turn split even more. Some scientists feared that the process would go on forever. The USA managed to develop such a bomb in 1945. It only had enough material to make several, including one for a test. The first test in the American state of New Mexico – witnessed by only a few military officials and scientists – proved its power. Within weeks the USA used two such bombs against Japan (see page 10–11). And, as all the world's scientists had predicted, the war was over within days.

The atomic bomb dropped on Hiroshima flattened the city and killed 78,000 people.

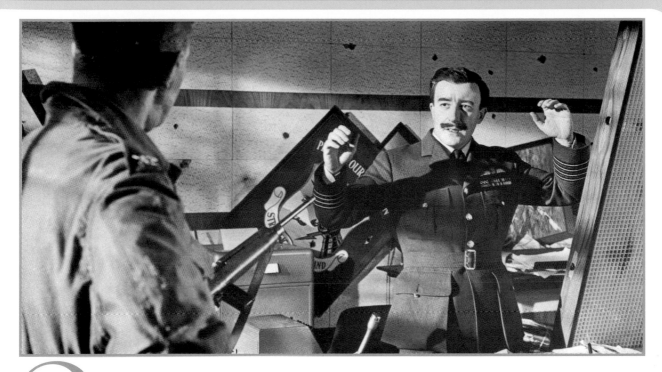

Some Cold War films such as *Dr Strangelove*, tapped people's fears of nuclear war.

After the war there was serious disagreement and debate about atomic weapons. In 1946, Bernard Baruch, a US representative to the **United Nations** even proposed an international agreement to destroy all atomic weapons. At that time the **Cold War** was just beginning and although the USA was the only country with atomic weapons, the Soviet representative **vetoed** this proposal.

Joining the 'club'

Luckily for the world, Germany never did develop the atomic bomb during the Second World War. But in the years after the war, several countries did – including the Soviet Union, France, the UK and China. By and large, these countries considered the weapons too powerful to be used in attack, and thought of them only as defensive weapons. In a sense, they had formed a 'club', and had to decide on rules about how these weapons could be used, limited or destroyed.

From the 1950s to the present day these countries have tried to stick within agreed limits about how the weapons would be produced and tested. But other countries have now shown that they can produce such weapons. Some, including Israel, India and Pakistan, are in 'hot spots' of the world, where war is possible, and it becomes very worrying to consider what would happen if they were to use such weapons.

Whose hand is on the trigger?

More worrying still is the fear that **terrorist** groups might get hold of these weapons. Whereas governments can agree among themselves about who holds how many weapons, a terrorist group is unlikely to announce that it has got hold of such a bomb. It might just decide to use one as a surprise. So even though the original fear – that the USA or the Soviet Union would use nuclear weapons during the Cold War – is over, a much greater fear remains. It is the fear of the unknown.

Ending conflicts

This book has looked at many aspects of war and the way it is conducted. But what about bringing such conflicts to an end? This can be very difficult, even if both sides recognize how much they have suffered.

Usually, both sides agree to an **armistice**, which 'buys time' to set about agreeing on a more permanent end to the war. Then representatives from both sides sit down at a conference to agree to the exact terms, usually expressed in a document called a treaty. The treaty considers who should control which areas, sometimes changing borders between countries or making other changes to reflect the events of the war. There is bound to be a winner and loser in each war, and treaties reflect this fact. The most difficult goal for a treaty is to produce a conclusion that is acceptable to both parties. It is important not to allow revenge. The Treaty of Versailles (see opposite), for example, failed to do this and led indirectly to yet more bloodshed.

US military officials accepted Japan's surrender on 14 August 1945, ending the Second World War.

PEACE OR PUNISHMENT?

The Treaty of Versailles, signed in 1919, officially ended the **First World War**. Several of the victorious nations, notably Britain and France, insisted on punishing Germany, so the treaty put many limits on what Germany could and could not do after the war. Also, Germany had to pay these countries back in the form of ships, trains and even cattle. Germany faced a terrible burden already, and these requirements – a form of punishment – led to economic difficulties and a great sense of anger among the German public. Many claim that it led directly to the rise of Adolph Hitler and the **Second World War** less than twenty years later.

THE WAR THAT NEVER HAPPENED

Ending a war is one thing. But what about the **Cold War** (see pages 8–9), which wasn't a war like any other. Even now, experts disagree on how and why the Cold War ended. One group argues that the USA, by building up a huge amount of weapons, forced the Soviet Union to build a similar amount. In doing so it spent so much that it ran out of money. In other words, they believe that a hard approach was the right one. Others say that a series of treaties between the USA and the Soviet Union – all of which were intended to reduce the use of powerful weapons – made them less likely to wage war.

What do you think ended the Cold War?

Although most wars and conflicts end with a cease-fire and armistice, which pave the way for a permanent peace treaty, sometimes the two sides cannot agree on a way forward. The state of Israel became involved in wars with its Arab neighbours almost from the time it was established in 1948. It was only in 1979 that Israel was able to sign a peace treaty with one of these neighbours, Egypt. Since then Israel has made progress in overcoming its differences with the Palestinian people, differences that lie at the heart of its wars against Arab neighbours.

The Korean War, which was fought between 1950 and 1953, is another example of a dispute that has never fully ended. The two sides, North Korea and South Korea, agreed to an armistice in 1953. The armistice settled on a border between the two countries. However, it never developed into a full peace treaty and soldiers from the two countries have peered nervously across the border at each other for nearly fifty years.

War crimes

International organizations such as the **United Nations** try to set 'rules' about how wars are conducted. Wartime leaders who break these rules – by deliberately killing innocent people or by mistreating prisoners – are considered 'war criminals'. These leaders can face trial in an international courtroom. The most famous war trials were held in the German city of Nuremberg just after the end of the Second World War. It was there that many German wartime leaders were tried and convicted of terrible crimes, including the **genocide** of the Jewish people and other groups. More recently, similar international trials have looked at the role of military leaders during the wars in the former Yugoslavia in the 1990s.

'We have won the war. Now we must win the peace.'

(US President Harry S Truman at the end of the Second World War)

Keeping the peace

Many world leaders at the time of the **First World War** believed that they were fighting 'the war to end all wars'. That opinion changed by the end of the war in 1918, but there remained a sense that the world should at least try to unite in some way for peace. It was this hope that lay behind the formation of the League of Nations in 1919. This group of countries, which included 63 of the world's nations over its 26-year history, tried to stop its members from going to war with each other. Considering that nearly every member joined with the memory of the First World War still fresh, why then did the League fail to prevent the **Second World War**?

Learning from mistakes

One reason is that the USA never became a member. Also, many members chose to ignore the League's wishes or to leave the League itself if they were criticized too strongly. In this respect, the league could only solve small matters, such as minor disputes over borders in Europe and South America.

Even before the Second World War ended, many countries were trying to build a stronger organization which would succeed where the League of Nations failed. This time, in the forming of the **United Nations** (UN), the USA not only joined the organization, it played a leading part in its development. It has many branches that work to improve living conditions, health and education in various parts of the world, but one of its chief roles is as a peacekeeper.

The blue helmets

The UN sends peacekeeping forces to troubled areas where two or more countries agree to try to find peace. UN member-countries volunteer their troops for this role – the UN has no army of its own. The soldiers wear their national uniforms, but on their heads they wear a blue helmet or beret with the UN symbol. Since their first mission to the Middle East in 1948, the peacekeepers have been involved in 49 missions, with troops supplied by 118 nations over the years. They have been involved in many of the world's 'hot spots' in that time, including missions to the former Yugoslavia, Congo and East Timor.

UN peacekeepers have strict orders in each mission. Most importantly, they must be **neutral**, and they have strict orders about the use of weapons. Normally they are only allowed to fire if they are fired upon. The peacekeepers' job is to maintain peace, and not to fan the flames of hatred. They often remain in a region after the fighting has stopped, helping the countries build new forms of fair government, as well as helping with day-to-day matters such as police work and medical treatment.

A step further

The UN peacekeepers have their critics, however. People argue that some UN missions have been badly planned and poorly carried out. Some UN troops look back on their involvement and argue that being neutral isn't always the right policy – in some cases there is a right and wrong

to the dispute. In Sierra Leone, an African country torn apart by a **civil war** in 1999–2000, UN troops were kidnapped and killed while remaining neutral. UN **Secretary-General** Kofi Annan has suggested that these UN forces should drop the need to be neutral in every case, in order to promote a fairer peace.

One solution to this problem, supported by Annan, is to use groups other than the UN to help in some disputes. Many world regions have local organizations that could supply troops to keep the peace. These soldiers would be more familiar with the people and their customs, as well as with the landscape – and perhaps they would be able to find peaceful solutions more easily.

> '[The aim of the United Nations] is to save succeeding generations from the **scourge** of war, which… has brought untold sorrow to mankind.'
>
> (from the United Nations **charter**)

Sierra Leone, with its heavily armed rival factions, has proved to be one of the most difficult tests for UN peacekeepers (above).

UN peacekeepers have patrolled the border in Cyprus since 1964 (right).

Wars of the future?

Wars and conflicts have been a part of human life throughout history. If the 20th century taught us anything, it is that it is hard to predict anything about wars. The **First World War**, which at the time was called the 'war to end all wars', led to another, even larger war within two decades. The terrible loss of life during the **Second World War** made the world's most powerful countries think hard about becoming involved in future large-scale conflicts – with nuclear weapons involved, a third world war would certainly be the last. Finally, the end of the **Cold War** brought increased wealth and new freedom to many countries, but it has also unleashed some age-old **ethnic** hatreds. International efforts to control the warfare have failed miserably, but they have at least managed to avoid another world war. There will certainly be more disputes in the future, but there are questions about how they will develop.

Will the **United Nations** (UN) (see pages 40–41) change its **strategy** and fall in with one side or the other in future conflicts? Will regional groups help the UN and even begin to replace it as a peacekeeping force? Will the initial conflicts following the end of the Cold War settle down? Will nuclear weapons become more easily available, both to countries and to terrorists?

'Smart bombs' and wise plans?

Nuclear weapons represent just one element in the choice of weapons available today, providing a country has enough money to make or buy them. The world has seen some of these in action in recent conflicts. Computer-guided bombs, known as 'smart bombs', enabled UN forces to defeat Iraq after it had tried to take over its neighbour Kuwait in 1990–91. Stealth bombers can fly low and quickly over enemy territory, using special paints and designs to avoid being picked up on radar screens (device which tracks objects by radio waves). Small nuclear weapons can destroy a limited area and neutron bombs can destroy all life in an area, while leaving buildings untouched. And although the 'Star Wars' plan (see pages 14–15) has been set aside, a smaller version was proposed by US President Bill Clinton in 2000. He was offering other countries – not simply the USA – protection against attack. But as with the earlier system, critics have argued that it gives the USA a chance to launch attacks without fear of being attacked in return.

Of course it is hard to say whether any of these weapons will be used in real combat in the future, or whether just knowing they exist – as the world knew about nuclear weapons during the Cold War – will help to prevent conflicts.

Familiar stories

The new century began just as the old one ended, with new nations emerging, and old ones regaining their independence. It seems as though local wars, between different ethnic groups, will be a feature of the next century. The trend has already been established.

The UN established 13 peacekeeping operations in the first 40 years of its existence (to 1988), but since then has launched 36 new missions.

So there are reasons to believe that human beings haven't really changed and that they keep on repeating their old mistakes. On the other hand there are reasons for hope. New weapons can be

The US stealth bomber, designed to fly undetected by radar, is an example of how weapons now rely heavily on technology.

used for peace. And, if the world's two most powerful countries – the USA and Russia – continue to co-operate, then they can join to promote peace, rather than threatening the world as they once did.

Glossary

Allied Forces combined armies of the Allies

Allies in the Second World War, countries (including the UK, USA and Soviet Union) that united against Germany, Italy and Japan

ambush sudden, unexpected attack

apartheid system of government rules that keep racial groups separate

archaeologist someone who studies evidence from the past to learn about ancient humans

armistice an agreed, but temporary, stop in fighting, in order for countries to discuss peace

atheism belief that there is no God

atomic weapon weapon that uses the power of a split atom to release large amounts of destructive energy

barbarian someone who is considered to be a savage

cause beliefs and ideals of a group

charter an organization's set of principles, written down

civilian someone who is not involved in the military; the vast majority of the public are civilians

civil war war between two or more groups within a country

Cold War period (1945–91) during which the USA and its allies were prepared to fight the Soviet Union and its communist allies

colony region that is ruled by a powerful foreign country

communist system of rule that calls for common ownership of property and companies

constitution written code of a country, which spells out who should have which responsibility

democratic describes a political system that allows all people an equal say in how they are governed

empire group of countries ruled by a single powerful country or government

ethnic to do with the way a particular group of people have a common language, culture and history

feudal concerning the system of government in the Middle Ages, in which farmers rented land from local noblemen

First World War war (1914–18), fought largely in Europe, between Germany, Austria and Hungary on one side and the UK, France, Russia and the USA on the other

free enterprise system of government opposed to communism, in which private individuals can own property and companies

free market system of government that allows people to own property and factories

genocide deliberate killing of a large group of people

guerrilla fighting in small armed bands, as opposed to large armies, making surprise attacks on the enemy

ideology system of ideas that a group of people (a nation or political movement) believes in

Industrial Revolution period in the 18th and 19th centuries when new types of machines were developed to produce goods

infidel insulting term to describe a person who believes in a different religion to yours, and is therefore considered less worthy

intercept to stop or interrupt the progress of something or someone

irrigation system that brings flowing water to farming areas

Islam religious faith as set down by the Prophet Muhammad in the 7th century

majority more than half of something

Middle Ages period in Europe, roughly between the 5th century and the 15th century

morale degree of confidence and happiness

Muslim follower of the Islamic faith

negotiations peaceful discussions to resolve a dispute

neutral taking neither side in a conflict

Parliament place where elected British officials decide on how the country is run

propaganda information that changes or ignores the truth to persuade people to think in a certain way

rebellion struggle against an established government or political system

Red Cross charitable organization (operating under the name the Red Crescent in Muslim countries) that provides much-needed medical and development assistance in 176 countries where people have suffered from natural disasters as well as destructive conflicts

refugee someone who is driven away from where they live because of fighting

revolution act of getting rid of an unwanted government by a group of people representing the overall population

scapegoat someone who is blamed (unfairly) when things go wrong

scourge something or someone that makes life horrible

secede to withdraw from, in order to be independent

Second World War war (1939–45), fought in many areas of the world, in which the UK, USA, Soviet Union and other Allies defeated Germany, Japan and their allies

Secretary-General person who leads the Secretariat, one of the most important departments of the United Nations

skirmish small battle

strategy long-term plans to achieve a goal

superpower one of the two countries (the USA and the Soviet Union) that were very powerful during the Cold War

tactic short-term plan to achieve a goal

terrorism use of illegal weapons or violence (or the threat of using them) to force a government to give in on a particular issue

tolerant able or willing to accept others

undemocratic describes a political system that fails to allow all people an equal say in how they are governed

United Nations international organization of 188 member-states that aims to promote peace, respect freedom and end conflict around the world

veto to vote against something

Contacts and helplines

There are many ways to learn more about war and conflict. Some of the best sources of information are on websites that supply detailed accounts of the history, extent and future of warfare. Other sites are devoted to conflict studies and peacekeeping. These concentrate on the reasons why people go to war and attempt to find ways of avoiding conflicts, or at least settling them peacefully. Listed below are several of the most useful websites, along with a brief description of their aims and content. Each of these sites is also a jumping-off point, allowing you to use their suggested links to find yet more websites devoted to similar subjects.

Military history and international affairs

COMMISSION ON GLOBAL GOVERNANCE

www.cgg.ch/chapt3.htm
This commission, with high-level members currently or formerly involved in world leadership roles, examines trends in world affairs and tries to prevent conflicts from beginning. It also provides useful links to similar websites.

UNITED NATIONS

www.UN.org
This main UN website has many links to pages dealing with its peacekeeping operations. There are full listings of all UN missions along with maps, participating nations and mission briefings.

WWW SITES FOR HISTORIANS

www.hist.unt.edu/09-www.htm
This is one of the most comprehensive of all websites devoted to military history. It has detailed accounts of military conflicts since written records began, including many pages concerning the world wars and other major conflicts of the 20th century. In addition, there are links to various military museums and exhibitions, such as the Imperial War Museum and the US Air Force Museum.

Emergency assistance sites

INTERNATIONAL COMMITTEE OF THE RED CROSS AND RED CRESCENT (ICRC)

www.icrc.org
The Red Cross, which operates under the name the Red Crescent in Muslim countries, provides much-needed medical and development assistance in 176 countries where people have suffered from natural disasters as well as destructive conflicts.

MEDICINS SANS FRONTIERES

www.msf.org
Medecins sans Frontieres (MSF) – meaning 'doctors without borders' – has been sending doctors and other medical staff to conflict areas around the world since 1971. MSF teams are all volunteers and risk their lives in some 80 countries.

Campaigning sites

CAMPAIGN FOR NUCLEAR DISARMAMENT (CND)

www.cnduk.org
CND has been raising public awareness about the dangers and expense of nuclear weapons since the tense days of the Cold War. Its website provides a history of the organization as well as helpful links to other sites dealing with weapon control.

INTERNATIONAL CAMPAIGN TO BAN LANDMINES (ICBL)

www.icbl.org
ICBL concentrates its efforts on ridding the world of landmines, weapons that wound and kill hundreds of innocent people each year – even years after conflicts have ended. It was awarded the Nobel Peace Prize in 1997.

INTERNATIONAL PHYSICIANS FOR THE PREVENTION OF NUCLEAR WAR (IPPNW)

www.ippnw.org
Awarded the Nobel Peace Prize in 1985, is composed of doctors from around the world with a shared aim: 'to promote non-violent conflict resolution and to minimize the effects of war on health, development and the environment.'

In Australia

AUSTRALIAN RED CROSS

National Resource Centre
155 Pelham Street
Carlton
VIC 3053
www.redcross.org.au
(access to state divisions provided at this address)

AUSTRALIAN WAR MEMORIAL

GPO Box 345
Canberra
ACT 2601

Treloar Crescent
Campbell
ACT 2612
2 6243 4211
www.awm.gov.au

Further reading

100 Military Leaders Who Shaped the World
Samuel Willard Crompton
Bluewood, 1999

Ancient Weapons and Warfare (Exploring History)
Will Fowler
Lorenz, 1999

A Soldier's Life: A Visual History of Soldiers through the Ages
Andrew Robertshaw
Heinemann Library, 1997

Hostage to War: A True Story
Tatiana Vasileva
Collins Educational, 1999

No Pretty Pictures: A Child of War
Anita Lobel
Avon Books, 2000

Organizations that help the world: United Nations
Michael Pollard
Prentice-Hall & IBD, 1994

Origins of War: From the Stone Age to Alexander the Great
Arthur Ferrill
Denver, CO: Westview, 1997

To End a War
Richard Holbrooke
Random House, 1999

Voices from Vietnam
Barry Denenberg
New York, NY: Scholastic, 1997

Wartime Whiffs (Smelly Old History)
Mary J Dobson
Oxford University Press, 1998

Index